taking tea

IN BELIZE

CREATING HEART CONNECTIONS
WITH OUR BROTHERS AND SISTERS
AT KOINONIA MINISTRIES

I first heard the expression "taking tea" when our daughter Rachel returned home after an eight month mission trip in Nairobi. Here, several times a day, everyone stops what they are doing to share a cup of tea and conversation with those they are with at the time. They call this tradition "taking tea."

From the moment I first heard of taking tea, I have desired to be more intentional about making heart connections with others over a cup of tea or coffee. In a world where we are more connected than ever - thanks to technology - we have an epidemic of loneliness. How can this be? Social media and other forms of technology, such as texting, often provide a false sense of connection. We were created by God to meet face-to-face, to hear human voices, to experience the energy that is found in the gathering of others. There is good in technology of course, but there is simply no substitution for direct human connection.

A group of us recently traveled to Belize on a mission trip. Our church has had a relationship with our friends at Koinonia Ministries for many years. I had heard many stories of our brothers and sisters in Christ there, but had never experienced time in Belize myself. From the moment the minister at our church, Pastor Troy, mentioned Pastor Ed and his heart for ministry, I knew I wanted to get to know this loving man of God who is all about connecting with others, quickly transforming strangers into family. How do they "take tea" at Koinonia Ministries?

The first night we arrived in Belize, Pastor Ed told us the painting of the church and the tutoring of the children were secondary to forming new friendships and making authentic connections - becoming family. Throughout the time we were there, he truly walked the talk of this initial conversation. There was no sense of being hurried by him to complete tasks. He was always willing to sit and have a conversation, as were his friends, family, and members of his congregation.

We were the ones who were more task-oriented, wanting to fulfill our responsibilities to our Belizean family. It was an interesting observation to make while we were there. We understood the urgency of completing tasks. We were only there for a few days and wanted to accomplish what we came to do, knowing the ongoing benefits and ministry that would last even after our departure from Belize. Even so, we experienced again and again the beauty of building relationships with others. Our friends in Belize have very little in the form of wealth and material possessions, yet they have what is truly important - faith in Jesus and their closely knit community of family and friends.

How are we doing at taking tea on a daily basis? I know for myself, I have to constantly remind myself that taking tea - forming true heart connections - is what is most important. Am I willing to put aside my personal agenda for the day as others approach me with the need to simply have someone listen?

The journal questions following each devotion are designed to invite you into our experience in Belize and prompt you to determine ways you can "take tea" right where you are.

The result of our team's time in Belize is this book of reflections, Taking Tea in Belize. Light a candle, curl up with a cup of tea or coffee, and share in our experience with our Koinonia family, as we once again "take tea" with God and with those we are called to serve.

"Share with the Lord's people who are in need. Practice hospitality."
- Romans 12:13

"As Jesus and his disciples were on their way, he came to a village where a woman named Matha opened her home to him." - Luke 10:38

On Saturday night the week we were in Belize, we had the privilege of eating dinner in several people's homes. Several of us ate at Dez's house. Dez had never participated with the mission teams that came because she works full-time. She decided to take the week off and spend the week with us. We were so glad she did! She was a blessing in many ways, including opening her home to us for a meal.

When we arrived, the food was already set out, awaiting our arrival. The table wasn't big enough to hold the four of us who came and her family, so she and her children stood at the counter behind us the entire time we were there. They never complained, but instead answered our questions about their lives and asked questions of us in return.

We cherished our time with Dez and her family. Several of us had other opportunities to bond with Dez, making leaving Belize especially difficult for this lovely lady and for the rest of us. We will long remember her selfless hospitality and willingness to share her story and her faith.

YOUR THOUGHTS

What is one way I can show hospitality today? Who could I invite for a meal or to simply share a cup of coffee and conversation?

Share lunch with friend !!

"This is how we know what love is: Jesus Christ laid down his life for us. And we ought to lay down our lives for one another." - 1 John 3:16

As mentioned in the introduction, Pastor Ed told us the painting of the church and tutoring were secondary to us getting to know one another and forming lifelong friendships. He truly lives his life believing what is meant to get done will get done. People first. Everything else of importance will be accomplished if it's meant to be. I saw him live this truth over and over again, as he was always willing to engage in conversation when approached.

Pastor Ed's first priority is feeding and tending to the children entrusted in his care. He told me there are many financial needs, such as paint for the church, but he simply trusts that God will supply the paint and the painters as he continues to feed the children.

He then said to me, "Here you all are! My answer to prayer." He stays true to his path and trusts God to take care of the rest. And he told me he is never disappointed. God always comes through.

YOUR THOUGHTS

What - or who - is my most important priority today?

_____

_____

_____

_____

_____

_____

_____

_____

_____

_____

_____

_____

_____

_____

_____

_____

_____

_____

_____

_____

"Finally, be strong in the Lord and in his mighty power. Put on the full armor of God, so that you can take your stand against the devil's schemes. For our struggle is not against flesh and blood, but against the rulers, against the authorities, against the powers of this dark world and against the spiritual forces of evil in the heavenly realms. Therefore, put on the full armor of God, so that when the day of evil comes, you may be able to stand your ground, and after you have done everything, to stand. Stand firm then, with the belt of truth buckled around your waist, with the breastplate of righteousness in place, and with your feet fitted with the readiness that comes from the gospel of peace. In addition to all this, take up the shield of faith, with which you can extinguish all the flaming flames of the evil one. Take the helmet of salvation and the sword of the Spirit, which is the word of God. And pray in the Spirit on all occasions with all kinds of prayers and requests. With this in mind, be alert and always keep praying for all the Lord's people." - Ephesians 6: 10-18

As mentioned in the previous devotion, Pastor Ed didn't spend time worrying about the future. He completely trusted God for his needs and the needs of those in his care. Time and time again, we witnessed Pastor Ed and our friends at Koinonia living out the above words from Ephesians. Their first response to challenges is to pray and then trust God to answer.

Months later, I still often reflect on this complete trust in God. Even though we know it's pointless to worry, worry is often our first response to life's challenges. In praying about this tendency to worry, God laid on my heart that every time we worry we should turn it into prayer. We know that of course, but it's not always easy to do. God reminded me when we turn our worries into prayers we are His warriors, transforming us from worriers to warriors. How awesome is that?!

The next time we worry, let's pray about our concerns. Rather than labeling ourselves as worriers or worry warts we can remind ourselves we are

YOUR THOUGHTS

Christ's warriors and label ourselves accordingly.

Through prayer, God transforms us from worriers to warriors.

What are you worried about today? Put on God's armor and pray. Invite other prayer warriors to pray with you and for you. God will transform you from a worrier to a warrior.

_____

_____

_____

_____

_____

_____

_____

_____

_____

_____

_____

_____

_____

_____

"Surely your goodness and love will follow me all the days of my life, and I will dwell in the house of the LORD forever." - Psalm 23:6

As we painted the church, there was worship music playing. At one point, the song,
"The Goodness of God" by CeCe Winans came on. I was singing along when I noticed a new friend Dez also singing along with the song.

Part of the lyrics of the song are:

"'Cause all my life You have been faithful
And all my life You have been so so good.
With every breath that I am able
Oh, I will sing of the goodness of God.

Your goodness is running after, it's running after me.
Your goodness is running after, it's running after me.
With my life laid down I surrender now.
I give you everything.
Your goodness is running after, it's running after me."

When the song ended, I went over and told Dez this was one of my favorite songs. She agreed and began to tell me her story about God's pursuit of her and her resulting belief in Him. Her life has not been easy. Her story of God's faithfulness with her and her family is a beautiful testimony of how God never gives up on us.

Even though Dez admitted she is on the quieter side, she was willing to open up her life to me, even though I was pretty much a stranger. After all, we had just gotten to Belize the day before. Not only did she open up to me, but I told her another friend who was part of our group, would also greatly benefit from hearing her story. She willingly shared her story a second time.

YOUR THOUGHTS

I noticed, due to our short time we had with our Belizean family, we delved quickly into deep conversation about our lives and about our faith with one another. There wasn't a lot of time for superficial conversation. We wanted to get to know one another quickly, knowing we only had a few days to establish lasting friendships and relationships. Our conversations, not only with Dez, but with the others in our group, began friendships and strengthened friendships that have continued even after we returned home.

Whose story could I listen to today? In what way(s) can I share my own story in order to encourage others?

_____

_____

_____

_____

_____

_____

_____

_____

_____

_____

_____

"And now we are brothers and sisters in God's family because of the blood of Jesus. -Hebrews 10:19 (TPT)

For whoever does the will of my Father in heaven is my brother and sister and mother." - Matthew 12:50

In conversation with Dez one day, she mentioned the women don't address each other by name without adding "sister." She couldn't even imagine addressing another woman without adding sister to her title. Thanks to sister Dez, several of us also began to address each other this way and it has stuck. There is something about addressing one another as sisters that adds a sense of being a true family, which of course we are inJeses.

Many people feel lonely and isolated today. Maybe they have lost mothers and fathers, sisters, and brothers to death, or due to family division of some kind. What would happen if we "adopted" others as brothers and sisters into our families? After all, God calls us to be brothers and sisters in Christ, loving one another and working together, spreading the good news of the gospel.

We can invite someone in for a meal, make a phone call or send a card to let that person know we are thinking about them, celebrate their birthday or other special occasion, invite them to a movie or out to dinner. The possibilities are endless. A small act can go a long way in reminding someone he or she is important and special to us.

YOUR · THOUGHTS

s there someone I know who is feeling lonely? Am I willing to "adopt" this
person as a sister or brother in Christ? If so, what would that look like?Maybe
you are the one feeling lonely. If so, who could you reach out to?

_____

_____

_____

_____

_____

_____

_____

_____

_____

_____

_____

_____

_____

_____

_____

_____

_____

_____

"Come, let us sing for joy to the LORD; let us shout aloud to the Rock of our salvation. Let us come before him with thanksgiving and extol him with music and song. For the LORD is the great God, the great King above all gods." - Psalm 95:1-3

On Sunday we sang, "God of This City" by Chris Tomlin at the church service, mostly in English and then repeating the chorus in Spanish, honoring our Belizean friends. On our last night in Belize, we had dinner at an outside restaurant. I sat next to Pastor Carlos. After our meal, he began singing "God of this City." I quickly joined him. He then asked me to sing the chorus. As I did, he sang over me in Spanish. The blending of our voices was beautiful - a true taste of Heaven. I wonder if in Heaven many different languages will be spoken and we will all understand one another.

The chorus of "God of This City" goes:

"There is no one like our God
There is no one like our God

Greater things are yet to come
And greater things are still to be done in this city.
Greater things are yet to come.
Greater things are still to be done here."

After we sang, both of us prayed a blessing over the great country of Belize. What a beautiful experience! We often talked about the veil of Heaven being thin during our time in Belize. This time with Pastor Carlos was definitely one of those times for me.

YOUR THOUGHTS

How does song enable me to experience the "thin veil of Heaven" in my life? What part of the world could I specifically pray for today?

_____

_____

_____

_____

_____

_____

_____

_____

_____

_____

_____

_____

_____

_____

_____

_____

_____

_____

_____

"Consequently, you are no longer foreigners and strangers, but fellow citizens with God's people and also members of his household, built on the foundation of the apostles and prophets, with Christ Jesus himself as the chief cornerstone. In him the whole building is joined together and rises to become a holy temple in the Lord. And in him you too are being built together to become a dwelling in which God lives by his Spirit." - Ephesians 2: 19-22

There was no actual "tea" involved; do soda drinks count? ;) My daughter Deborah and I took tea with Dyna and Anamarylin the day we arrived.

When we finally all got through customs on our first day in Belize, everyone began boarding the two available vans that would bring our group from the Belize Airport to Koinonia Ministries in Orange Walk. Deborah and I soon realized the two vans were too full for us so we rode in the only remaining vehicle, the church's pick up truck. We jumped in the back seat. Mind you it was in the high 80's that day, I don't think the AC was working in the truck and the back seat was worn down to the bare foam stuffing. I was thinking, oh my, what did we get ourselves into?

That thought soon passed as I started my usual habit when I meet new people, of asking questions. We soon found out that Dyna spoke, or understood zero English, so Anamarylin was her interpreter. We fired a lot of questions at her. We found out how old she was, that she was a senior in high school, and had plans to go on to college. In fact, she had already been taking some classes at the local community college. We also learned that she and her younger brother spent all but their sleeping hours at the church and with the pastor's family, due to challenges in her family. She said was a Christian, but her family was not.

Sometimes she doesn't even wish to go home to sleep. But in spite of this, her faith in God shone through and we saw nothing but a positive spirit. We learned later that she is a main leader in the Sunday worship services. We were fortunate enough to experience her leadership with the youth while we were there. She is filled with the Holy Spirit.

YOUR THOUGHTS

We got to know Dyna during the week, as she cooked ALL of our meals and served with love. She is a beautiful soul. Our hour-long ride turned out to be an introduction to what we were to experience during the five days with these beautiful Christian people and was the best "cup of tea ever."

Where do I notice Christ's leadership in others? Who could I thank for the leadership and selfless service he or she provides?

_____

_____

_____

_____

_____

_____

_____

_____

_____

_____

_____

_____

_____

_____

"There is neither Jew nor Gentile, neither slave nor free, neither male nor female, for you are all one in Christ Jesus." - Galatians 3:28

"So God created human beings in his own image, in the image of God he created them; male and female he created them." - Genesis 1:27

What comes to mind most from the trip was the sameness of humanity. We try to act like we are all so different and even choose to like/dislike those differences; yet, most of us are out in the world making the best of circumstances and trying to be good people.

Being kind doesn't require money, a job, status, plumbing, electricity......at the base of all of us is an attempt to be good people.

The diversity of the people in the group and in the community, the diversity of the wealth and amenities were evident. When we show love and kindness to one another, the differences in each other are less evident. Jesus was seen in each person we connected with during our time in Belize.

YOUR THOUGHTS

Who can I demonstrate kindness to today?

"Now when Jesus returned, a crowd welcomed him, for they were all expecting him. Then a man named Jairus, a synagogue leader, came and fell at Jesus' feet, pleading with him to come to his house because his only daughter, a girl of about twelve, was dying.

As Jesus was on his way, the crowds almost crushed him. And a woman was there who had been subject to bleeding for twelve years, but no one could heal her. She came up behind him and touched the edge of his cloak, and immediately her bleeding stopped.

'Who touched me?' Jesus asked.

When they all denied it, Peter said, 'Master, the people are crowding and pressing against you.'

But Jesus said, 'Someone touched me; I know that power has gone out from me.'

Then the woman, seeing that she could not go unnoticed, came trembling and fell at his feet. In the presence of all the people, she told why she had touched him and how she had been instantly healed. Then he said to her, 'Daughter, your faith has healed you. Go in peace.'

While Jesus was still speaking, someone came from the house of Jairus, the synagogue leader. 'Your daughter is dead,' he said. 'Don't bother the teacher anymore.'

Hearing this, Jesus said to Jairus, 'Don't be afraid; just believe, and she will be healed." - Luke 8: 40-50

There was never a sense of being rushed during our time in Belize. Even though we joked about being on Belizean time, many of us found a sense of peace at the change of pace.

There is no Bible verse that says, "Jesus hurried." Jesus kept in step with God's timing, no matter what else was going on around Him. The above Scripture gives us a perfect picture of Jesus's pace. The crowds are crushing Him; yet He was never frazzled. Even when Jairus tells Jesus his daughter is dying, Jesus stops when a woman touches his robe and is healed. He tends to the woman as if she is the only person present at the moment. He completely trusts that God will care for Jairus's daughter until He can get to her. At the moment, the woman who has been healed is His top priority.

How can I ensure everyone I encounter today feels truly seen and valued?

"'Martha, Martha,' the Lord answered, 'you are worried and upset about many things, but few things are needed—or indeed only one. Mary has chosen what is better, and it will not be taken away from her.'" - Luke 10:41-42

God is omnipotent. He is not bound by time. He is able to bend time and events in our favor. We can accomplish more in less time when we offer ourselves fully to God in rich communion.

We experienced the truth of God's omnipotence time and again, as we observed our Belizean friends' complete trust in God's goodness and faithfulness. There was a peace in their spirits as they leaned into God's perfect will and timing.

 # YOUR THOUGHTS

Where can I slow down in my life so I can experience God's peace and presence?

_____

_____

_____

_____

_____

_____

_____

_____

_____

_____

_____

_____

_____

_____

_____

_____

_____

_____

"Two are better than one, because they have a good return for their labor. If they fall down, they can help each other up." - Ecclesiastes 4:9-10

There is a purposeful pace to life. Because our days are focused solely on the task at hand (serving together at Koinonia), we have a clarity of purpose for our actions and time.

Some things I especially appreciate about our Koinonia Family are:

• Community - That church family really cares for each other.
• A broader definition of family - People look after one another.
• Provision - One of Pastor Ed's common sayings is "We believe God that..." and it usually has to do with God's provision for how they are hoping to serve God.
• Beauty - A beautiful country with beautiful people.

YOUR THOUGHTS

Where am I building a sense of community in my life?

"And do not forget to do good and to share with others, for with such sacrifices God is pleased." - Hebrews 13:16

There are tuition costs to attend school. No one is kicked out if they can't pay. However, after eighth grade, you have to pay $700.00 a year to attend school and your bill from the previous years follows you.

One woman lives on the property rent free. The money she would pay for rent goes for her child's schooling. This same woman lived in an extremely abusive situation. Pastor Ed provided a place to stay for her and also hired her to do all of their cooking.

Our Koinonia family serves 30 students lunch every day who can't afford lunch at school. They are constantly on the lookout for those who are struggling, especially the children. When they see a need, they don't hesitate to share what they have, trusting that God will multiply the little they have to give. He will take their small offerings and cover everyone under their care.

YOUR THOUGHTS

Who can I share the resources I have been gifted with today?

_____

_____

_____

_____

_____

_____

_____

_____

_____

_____

_____

_____

_____

_____

_____

_____

_____

_____

"All the believers were together and had everything in common. They sold property and possessions to give to anyone who had need. Every day they continued to meet together in the temple courts. They broke bread in their homes and ate together with glad and sincere hearts, praising God and enjoying the favor of all the people. And the Lord added to their number daily those who were being saved." Acts 2:44-47

Just imagine...a community where everyone

• Shows love and compassion for all
• Cares for each other
• Works together as one big family
• Knows the needs of others and helps
• Trusts the youth to be leaders
• Shares what they have
• Is grateful for what they have
• Feeds the souls of others
• Through their actions shows the Holy Spirit is working in each one of them
• Enjoys the beauty found in each other
• Believes in the joyful awe of Jesus

We found these traits in our Koinonia family in Orange Walk, Belize.

YOUR THOUGHTS

How can we create a similar community right where we are?

"Jesus said, 'Let the little children come to me, and do not hinder them, for the kingdom of heaven belongs to such as these.'" - Matthew 19:14

Pastor Ed felt a strong call from God to minister to the children in Orange Walk. He was strongly criticized by others, as they wondered how he could sustain a ministry to children. They would not have financial means to support the ministry. Pastor Ed didn't have the answers, but knew this was what God was calling him to do and followed his heart.

He involved the children early on in his ministry. Those same little children helping to pour cement for the physical foundation of the church have become - alongside Christ -the spiritual foundation of the church. They are now teenagers and are the leaders of the church. They are fully invested in Koinonia Ministries.

YOUR THOUGHTS

What is God calling me to do?

"Jesus replied, 'Love the Lord your God with all your heart and with all your soul and with all your mind.' This is the first and greatest commandment. And the second is like it: 'Love your neighbor as yourself.'" -Matthew 22:37-39

The children in Belize are beautiful servants of God. They willingly served and cleaned up at the dinners we were invited to at various homes. They led worship and helped out at the youth service.

Their lives are not easy by any stretch of the imagination, but we would never have known that if we hadn't been told. There is joy on their faces from serving Jesus and others. We were very impressed by their maturity, leadership, and giving spirits.

So many of our youth here in the states are crippled by anxiety and depression. I wonder if they had more opportunities to serve others - if they immersed themselves in service - if they would finally escape the chains of the mental health challenges they face. This is not only true for our young people, but for each one of us. God calls us to love others - not only because it's the right thing to do - but because He knows as we reach out to one another in service, our souls are healed and nourished.

We spend so much time asking ourselves if we are happy and if our needs are being met. As soon as we ask ourselves those questions, we find reasons we aren't happy and seek ways to be "happier." Maybe a better question to ask is who we can serve out of the abundance God has provided.

YOUR THOUGHTS

Who can I serve today out of the abundance God has provided for me? Abundance can be monetary, but it also includes our time and talents.

"'Do not store up for yourselves treasures on earth, where moth and rust destroy, and where thieves break in and steal. But store up for yourselves treasures in heaven, where moths and rust do not destroy, and where thieves do not break in and steal. For where your treasure is, there your heart will be also.'" - Matthew 6:19-21

Our friends in Belize are not wealthy by the world's standards, but they are rich in community and in their love and care for one another. I was struck by their generosity with everyone. The little they had they freely shared with us and with everyone around them.

Here in America, we have wealth, but often lack community. We hold on tightly to our money and our possessions. We struggle with anxiety, depression, and loneliness. I couldn't help thinking during my time with my Koinonia family, that my Belizean friends might be poor in the things of this world, but they are rich in what matters most: their love for God and for one another.

 YOUR THOUGHTS

In what ways am I rich in the things that matter the most?

"...Instead, be filled with the Spirit, speaking to one another with psalms, hymns and songs from the Spirit. Sing and make music from your heart to the Lord, always giving thanks to God the Father for everything, in the name of our Lord Jesus Christ."
- Ephesians 5:18b-20

There was lots of singing and dancing during our time in Belize. We loved this joyous expression of praise to God!

We noticed people would break into song spontaneously wherever they were doing, whatever was happening. One of these times was when we were driving. Now, driving even in the U.S. can be stressful, but driving in Belize holds its own challenges. For example, there are often dogs lying in the road. When we first witnessed this, we thought the poor animal had been hit by a car. We soon realized the dogs were lazily sleeping in the streets. Unfazed, Pastor Ed Pastor Carlos simply carefully approached the dogs until they slowly got up and moved out of the road.

The roads themselves are not in great condition, although they are not so different from the condition of our roads here. There are hidden speed bumps everywhere and very few street signs and traffic lights. People constantly cut our drivers off. I remarked several times that I was glad I didn't have to drive. Whenever something crazy happened, our Belizean friends spontaneously broke into a praise song, albeit many times tinged with a hint of frustration. It was actually quite funny and they often laughed after their melodic outburst.

I thought to myself how freeing it would be to adopt this reaction to different challenges at home.

YOUR THOUGHTS

When do I find myself getting frustrated? What would happen if I burst into songs of praise at these times? How would songs of praise change my perspective of the situation?

_____

_____

_____

_____

_____

_____

_____

_____

_____

_____

_____

_____

_____

_____

_____

_____

_____

_____

"How beautiful are the feet of those who bring good news!" - Romans 10:15

On the last night we were all together in Belize, Pastor Ed had those of us from First Presbyterian Church make a circle. He and his family surrounded us. As Pastor Ed prayed over us, his friends and family also prayed aloud. We couldn't discern their words, but they sounded like angels. It was the most profound spiritual experience I have ever had!

As Christ's followers, we have the privilege of telling others about Jesus' sacrifice on the cross and resurrection. The captives of sin are set free thanks to Jesus. When we spread this message, we are beautiful and blessed. As Pastor Ed spoke the words of Romans 10:15 over us, he touched each of our feet. We sensed God's Spirit in a powerful way. This sacred encounter will forever be etched in my heart.

YOUR THOUGHTS

Who could I share a word of encouragement with today as I share the gospel of God's love through Christ Jesus?

_____

_____

_____

_____

_____

_____

_____

_____

_____

_____

_____

_____

_____

_____

_____

_____

_____

"Let your conversation be always full of grace, seasoned with salt, so that you may know how to answer everyone." - Colossians 4:6

In the above verse, the Apostle Paul is referring to the importance of words being a delight to those we are engaging in conversation. Our words can be used as a preservative, building and strengthening relationships.

Many of us often engage in surface conversation, talking about the weather or other subjects of little importance. Our answers to how we are doing are often simply, "fine," "okay," or "great, thanks for asking," and we are on our way. We may or may not ask how the other person is doing.

In Belize, there wasn't time for surface conversation. We had very little time - six days -to get to know our new friends. There was an urgency in diving deep into matters of the heart. We wanted to hear their stories and they in turn, wanted to hear ours. I learned more about our new friends in a matter of days than I know about many of my friends here in the states. I, in turn, shared my own stories, some of which I had told very few people in my life.

There was a deep level of sharing I think many of us crave and maybe never truly experience. I found myself wondering how we could adopt these "taking tea" moments - create heart connections - back home in Michigan. It is definitely something to contemplate and to be in prayer about. Lifelong friendships were formed in a matter of days, thanks to the safe, caring community we experienced with our friends at Koinonia Ministries.

YOUR THOUGHTS

What are some ways I can "take tea" - create heart connections - right where I am?

ACKNOWLEDGEMENTS

Members of the Belizean Mission Team

Karen Abraham
Kathy Alles
Patrick Duell
Naomi Force
Amy Geren
Jana Hazekamp
Troy Hauser-Brydon
Karen Losse
Karen Nienhouse
Sue Ochs
Nita Pellegrom
Betsy Planteroth
John Planteroth
Deborah Post
Hannah Post
Deb Stanley

Thank you all for your contribution to this book. It was wonderful to "take tea" with you as we spent time with our amazing Koinonia family! It was truly a life-changing experience of creating new friendships and strengthening friendships already in existence.

Thank you to Maegan Sadocha for once again sharing your gifts in creating my book covers, formatting, and uploading my book to Amazon. You are an incredible blessing in my life!

Made in United States
Cleveland, OH
07 November 2024

10504948R10029